# I Feel...

Words and pictures by

**DJ Corchin**

Sometimes I feel **happy**.

Sometimes I feel **sad.**

Sometimes I feel **angry** and want to be **bad**.

Sometimes I feel **jealous** and want what you have.

# Sometimes I'm **solid.**

But inside I'm **plaid.**

# Sometimes I'm **surprised**

or have some **self-doubt**.

Sometimes I'm **ashamed**...

or **annoyed,**
and I **pout.**

Sometimes I'm **disgusted** by something I see.

I might even **judge** you by what that might be.

Usually it's 'cause what
I see is in **me**.

Sometimes I'm **in love**.

Sometimes I'm **in awe.**

# Sometimes I'm **afraid**

of creatures that crawl.

Sometimes I feel **guilt**.

Sometimes I feel **pride.**

Sometimes I'm so **nervous**,
I eat all the pie.

Sometimes I **don't trust.**

Sometimes I feel **joy**.

Sometimes I'm **remorseful** 'cause I broke your new toy...

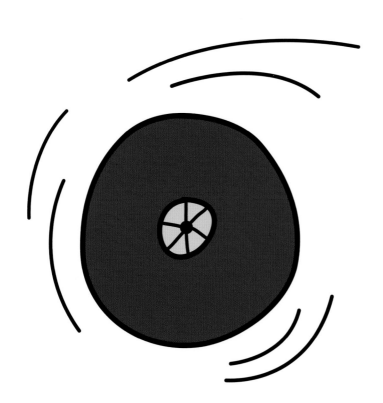

and not just a crack—I mean
**COMPLETELY** destroyed.

There's **one billion** feelings.
Which ones do I use?

Is it bad that I'm **honest** and completely **confused**?

So many **emotions**.
How do I deal?

I need to remember, it's **OK** that **I feel**.

# The
# I Feel...
## Children's Series

## There are so many feelings!
## It's hard to know where to start.

Acknowledging that it's perfectly normal to have so many different emotions (often at the same time) can be a productive first step to learning how to self-regulate, self-soothe, and start more meaningful conversations around emotional awareness.

**The I Feel... Children's Series** is designed to be a discussion starter between children, parents, teachers, and mental health professionals. Here are some additional questions and activities to do that can help further explore social-emotional awareness.

## Look at yourself in a mirror and ask:

1. Does my feeling have a name?

2. Do I feel more than one feeling?

3. What does someone's face look like when they are feeling this way?

4. Have I seen anyone else look this way?

5. Does my face look that way now?

6. Do I want to keep feeling this way?

7. If so, what can I do to keep feeling this way?

8. If not, what can I do to feel different?

9. What might my face look like if I felt something different?

## It is ALWAYS OK to ask someone for help when you are feeling bad.

The I Feel... Children's Series is a resource created to assist in discussions about emotional awareness.

Please seek the help of a trained mental healthcare professional and start a discussion today.

## Draw an I FEEL... face!

1. Think about how you feel right now. You're going to draw yourself!

2. Draw a circle or an oval on a piece of paper using a marker.

3. Look at yourself in a mirror or ask someone to take a picture of you.

4. Draw what your eyes look like. Are they wide open? Are they closed?

5. Draw your eyebrows. Do they go up or down?

6. Draw your nose. They come in all shapes and sizes!

7. Draw your mouth. Are your teeth showing? Do you have dimples?

8. Color away!

9. Write on the bottom, "I FEEL..." and then put the feeling you just drew.

## There are so many emotions!
## Which one do I feel?

## Make a feelings book:

1. Using the activity on the previous page, draw an I Feel... face for as many emotions as you can think of and collect them in a stack.

2. Arrange them in any order you like: alphabetical, by color, by fun feelings, by sad feelings, etc.

3. Use a hole punch (ask an adult for help if you need to) and punch eight holes on the left side of the stack.

4. Weave a piece of yarn through the holes and tie a knot on both ends.

5. When you're not sure what you're feeling, use your feelings book to look for ideas!

## Questions to start asking yourself about what you're feeling:

1. When I feel this way, do I want to be alone or with others?

2. Do I like feeling this way?

3. What does my body feel like when I feel this way?

4. Do I know anyone else who might feel the same?

5. What happened that made me feel this way?

6. Who can I talk to about how I feel?

# To Mom

Published by Sourcebooks eXplore, an imprint of Sourcebooks Kids
P.O. Box 4410, Naperville, Illinois 60567–4410
(630) 961-3900
sourcebookskids.com

Originally published in 2011 in the United States of America by The phazelFOZ Company, LLC.

Library of Congress Cataloging-in-Publication Data is on file with the publisher.

Source of Production: 1010 Printing Asia Limited, North Point, Hong Kong, China
Date of Production: July 2020
Run Number: 5019062

Printed and bound in China.
OGP 10 9 8 7 6 5 4 3 2 1